Henry Philip Tappan

A Discourse on the Death of Abraham Lincoln

Henry Philip Tappan

A Discourse on the Death of Abraham Lincoln

ISBN/EAN: 9783337401986

Printed in Europe, USA, Canada, Australia, Japan

Cover: Foto ©Thomas Meinert / pixelio.de

More available books at **www.hansebooks.com**

A DISCOURSE

ON THE DEATH OF

ABRAHAM LINCOLN

LATE PRESIDENT OF THE UNITED STATES OF AMERICA

DELIVERED TUESDAY MAY 2. 1865 IN THE
DOROTHEEN-CHURCH. BERLIN

BY

HENRY P. TAPPAN DD. LL. D.

BERLIN

PRINTED BY G. LANGE.

PREFACE.

More than half a century ago the rights of Free-Labor were acknowledged and established, in Prussia, by the Edict of Oct. 9. 1807.

By the law of March 9. 1857, the sublime principle, that no slave can set his foot on the soil of Prussia, can breathe the air of Prussia, was proclaimed. The moment he steps within the boundaries of Prussia, **he is free.**

For the rights of Free-Labor, and to banish from the soil and the air of America the foul and blighting taint of slavery, a dreadful war has been carried on for four years. At the close of this war, and in the very hour of victory and triumph, our great Leader has fallen, and sealed the great and holy cause with the blood of martyrdom.

The American Minister in Berlin, well known for his devotion to this cause, inviting the cooperation of Americans resident in Berlin, made arrangments for holding public funeral services in honor of the illustrious dead, and to afford a suitable opportunity for the public expression of a sympathy which seemed well nigh universal.

No official invitations were given, and the whole assemblage was voluntary. It was gratifying to find the Dorotheen-Church filled to its utmost capacity. The audience was composed of persons of all ranks and classes; a Representative of the King, the Prime Minister, other officers of the Government, members of the House of Representatives, Diplomatic Ministers of different nations, citizens of Berlin, strangers from other countries, and Americans.

ORDER OF THE FUNERAL SERVICES.

VOLUNTARY on the Organ.

CHORAL.
Jesus, meine Zuversicht,
Und mein Heiland ist im Leben!
Dieses weiss ich, sollte nicht
Sich mein Herz zufrieden geben?
Was die lange Todesnacht
Mir auch für Gedanken macht.

Jesus, er, mein Heiland, lebt,
Ich werd' auch das Leben schauen,
Sein, wo mein Erlöser lebt,
Warum sollte mir denn grauen?
Lässet auch ein Haupt sein Glied,
Welches es nicht nach sich zieht?

LESSON and PRAYER.

MUSIC.
Sei getreu bis in den Tod, so will ich dir die Krone
des Lebens geben.

Musik von Neithardt.

DISCOURSE
by Rev. H.P. Tappan, D.D. of New-York.

—

MUSIC.

Selig sind die Todten, die in dem Herrn sterben, sie ruhen von ihrer Arbeit.

Musik von Kähler,
für Männerstimmen von F. Schulz.

ADRESS by Rev. F. W. Krummacher, Th. D.,
Court-preacher at Potsdam.

CHORAL.

Seid getrost und hocherfreut,
Ihr seid alle Christi Glieder;
Gebt nicht Statt der Traurigkeit,
Sterbt ihr, Christus ruft euch wieder,
Wenn einst die Posaune klingt,
Die durch alle Gräber dringt.

BENEDICTION by Pastor Vater.

Amid all the convulsions of the World there goes forth a voice, as if music were changed into the waves of light, or, as if the waves of light were only the breath of Music — a voice consoling, soothing, commanding, *"Be still, and know that I am God"**).

If the Spirits, who surround the throne of God looking down upon the earth when its masses were upheaved and torn asunder by conflicting elements, were filled with dismay at the seeming chaotic confusion and ruin, then they heard the voice, "Be still, and know that I am God". And they became silent, and were comforted, and waited patiently. Then, in process of time the crust of the earth was fixed, and mountains and hills, and vallies and plains, and streams and rivers, and lakes and oceans appeared, and the earth was clothed with verdure, and became the beautiful and happy habitation of rejoicing creatures.

So, also, in the moral and political agitations of Mankind, society has often been shaken to its foundations, and persecution and woe and sorrow, wrath and war and tumult, terror and desolation appeared to be establishing their reign upon the earth. The sweep of the Barbarians from the North over the Roman Empire, the irruption fo the Ottomans, the conflicts of the Reformation, the thirty years war of Germany, the wars of Spain in the Netherlands, the civil wars of England extending through centuries until Magna Charta culminated in the Bill of

*) Psalm XLVI, 10.

Rights, the French Revolution, the wars in the time of Napoleon, presented such scenes of terror and desolation, and filled the hearts of Millions with dismay. But there were souls whom the voice, "Be still and know that I am God", penetrated; and they bore and had patience, they labored on in the cause of truth liberty and charity, and did not faint, and they had their reward: New energies of humanity came into being; fairer forms of civilisation appeared; and knowledge, liberty, and christianity were advanced.

The war of the American Revolution was a war of sorrow and suffering; but the results were glorious: the foundations of a new Empire of freedom were laid, and preparations made for a new and happier development of the human race. But the work of Washington was not complete. A portentous evil lingered upon the continent. The Declaration of Independence had affirmed "that all men are created equal; that they are endowed by their Creator with certain inalienable rights; that among these are life, liberty, and the pursuit of happiness": while under the Constitution of the United states slavery continued to exist. In our country the elements of an extreme democracy, and of an extreme despotism attempted to live together. The founders of the Constitution hoped that slavery would die out. It did die out in the northern states: it survived and increased in the southern states. Opposing forms of social life, opposing political ideas were the result. The "irrepressible conflict" spread and became more intense, until it broke out into open and bloody war.

During four years this war has prevailed. Who can adequately describe the sacrifices and sufferings of this war! Our land is filled with widows and orphans; in our dwellings are weeping, lamentation and woe; tens of thousands of our brave young men have fallen in battle;

tens of thousands have been starved to death in southern prisons; loyal households have been visited with outrage, plunder and murder, or have been driven away and hunted like the partridge upon the mountains; mutilated men are seen everywhere; and fair and fruitful fields have been reduced to desolation. While this war was in progress who can tell of the anxiety and dismay! Men's hearts failed them, and they grew pale with fearful forebodings. The triumph of our cause was despaired of at home and abroad. We were ridiculed and scorned as the *disunited* States. Multitudes in joy or in grief, according to their sympathies, looked upon the Great Republic as a failure. But above the noise of battle, and above all the weeping lamentation and woe, and above all fear and scorn, the serene voice still went forth, soothing, consoling, and commanding, "Be still and know that I am God". Our President heard the voice, and his tried commanders heard the voice, and the hosts of brave men in the field heard the voice, and the hosts of the people heard the voice. The *Nation* did not despair. The effort was renewed with unconquerable energy. The victory was won, and the cause of freedom and humanity has gloriously triumphed.

It was when the joy of victory was at its height, and all hearts were thrilled at the approach of peace; and when our good President indulging in no proud exultation and no vindictive feelings, but full of mercy and forgiveness, was intent upon plans of reconciliation, and of reconstructing the shattered Union; and when dreams of forgiveness, of injuries healed, of love revived, of brotherhood restored, and of the glorious and peaceful future of our country rose up before him: it was in these hours, fondly regarded as hours of returning peace and good will that conspiracy ripened, and

the hand of the assassin smote him to the earth. A new
and unexpected terror suddenly flashes into the eyes of
the people, a new and more poignant grief pierces their
hearts. We are now a nation of orphans: the Father of
his country is dead. Again the land is filled with weeping
lamentation and woe. It is a mingled storm of passion
that sweeps over the land: it is love, grief, despair, and
indignation.

But above this storm of passion the serene voice is
heard once more, consoling, soothing, and commanding,
"Be still and know that I am God". Believe ye people,
that God still reigns, and that his purposes embrace the
rights of humanity. Behind this new terror God's de-
livering angel stands with smiling face.

Who can say that this new lesson was not needed to
teach our country, and to teach the Nations, the utter
demoralisation, the barbarousness, the meanness, the in-
famy, the unscrupulous and unsparing ferocity of the
slave power?

Who can say, that this new lesson was not needed to
prevent the generosity and kindness which sprang up in
the path of victory from degenerating into a weakness
that might leave the country open to new perils, and
delay the full and perfect triumph of freedom and humanity? We might in our pity have taken the benumbed
serpent to our bosoms and have warmed it into activity, only to be stung afresh. But look at this long
train of Mourners! A funeral procession from Washington to Baltimore, from Baltimore to Philadelphia, from
Philadelphia to New York, from New York to Albany,
from Albany to Buffalo, from Buffalo to Cleveland, from
Cleveland to Columbus, from Columbus to Indianapolis,
from Indianapolis to Chicago, from Chicago to Spring-
field; one funeral procession eighteen hundred miles

long; weeping and indignant millions bearing the murdered President to his grave! We trust in God that there will break forth no wild spirit of vindictiveness. But, one thing is certain: this people is now nerved for all the duties of the hour. Not a trace of slavery or of the slave power will be left. There will be a stern purification of the land. Whatever is necessary for the security of the nation, the stability of the Union, the perfection of freedom, and the protection of all the rights of man, will be done. "Life, liberty, and the pursuit of happiness" will be guarded by adamantine shields.

One gracious fruit has already sprung from this great sorrow, and that is the sympathy of the nations. It is a spontaneous sympathy: it is a universal sympathy. Governments and peoples alike give expression to a deep and tender condolence. The multitude collected here to day is one of the manifestations of this generous and spontaneous sympathy. It is wonderful how grandly the virtues of this great and good but unpretending man stand up around his grave and make their irresistable appeal to all human hearts. His character is transparent: all read it: no one questions it. By his death, he has consecrated his country's cause afresh. Mankind look upon him as the martyr of Freedom and Mercy. He is the sanctified representative of his country's cause. In paying homage to his virtues, they pay homage to that cause. Around the grave of Lincoln, the nations of the Earth justify the struggle of America. The people and the Captain of the people are both glorified by his death. This lively sympathy, this generous and fitting homage draw the old and the new world into a fraternal embrace. Are not all prepared to say, America belongs not to itself alone: it belongs to the world, and now that it is purified it will play a grander part in illustrating and promoting the brotherhood of Nations?

And now assembled as we are Americans and Germans and individuals, also, of other nations, on an occasion so painful, and yet an occasion that is not without consolations, and fair promises, what can we do that will be more appropriate, or that will chime more harmoniously with the feelings which have drawn us together, than to bring before us the character of this man, and the nature and spirit of that cause in which he was the leader and to which he has fallen an honored victim, and last of all, the wisdom and fidelity with which he fulfilled his great and sacred trust?

Abraham Lincoln was a laborer, and the son of a laborer. He had few advantages of education. A pious mother taught him to read the Bible. This to him was much, for he never ceased to read it, and made it the man of his counsel and the light of his path. For short periods he attended a common school in Kentucky where he was born, and in Indiana to which State his father emigrated. But his education was essentially a self-education. His strong and supple arm felled the trees of the forest and opened the fair fields of pasturage and corn. He was a son of that beneficent industry which has made all the improvements of the world, created all the wealth and comforts of the world, and led on all the civilization and refinement of the world. While his arm wrought, his mind thought. He was a free man in the great wilderness. He was free to improve the earth, and to improve himself, and to take part in building up a new society. There is a wonderful stimulus in this freedom where so many possibilities are open before one. The far off settler in a western wilderness may amass property, take part in founding a community, become one of its pillars, and grow into a social moral and political power, an element of the great nation. Thus thousands and tens of thousands are developed, and the new States spring into being. Abraham Lincoln gifted with sagacity, honest and worthy aims, and steady perseverance, availed himself of every thing that could minister to his manhood, and faithfully met the claims of duty in the relations around him. He read books as he could find them, and sought for them as he wanted them. He became, early, a public man; and his reading was governed mainly by the exigencies of his life.

There are, in general, two forms of education: One is the regular and prescribed form of institutions of learning, where men are systematically trained to the acquisition of knowledge and to mental developement. The other is found in the relations, circumstances, events, exigencies, and duties of human life. He who has the good fortune to begin with the first, in order to become a practical and useful man must be moulded and finished by the second. The completeness of education lies in both. Under the second form, education has no limits, but grows with time and opportunities. He who has not the first may, through diligence, supply his deficiencies, by means of the second. He who has only the first, as a recluse student may advance knowledge, but cannot be a great actor in human life. Some of the greatest actors in public affairs have been formed in the second way. Richard Cobden, who has just passed away from us, was formed in this way. In our own history, Washington, Franklin, Jackson, and Henry Clay are noted examples. When a man's origin is lowly, it adds the more to his glory when he becomes a great man. Such an one absolutely conquers fortune. Abraham Lincoln labored with his hands in a community of laborers, who by labor were founding states. There was no imperial idleness. Every thing was done by hard, man ful, creative, productive labor. It was man asserting his lordship over nature.

Abraham Lincoln felt himself impelled to become one of the leading spirits of the West; and thus he grew to be a lawyer and a politician. He studied the history, the constitution and the laws of his country. He guided himself in his pursuit of knowledge by the wants of his position, and the wants of the community in which he lived. He gained knowledge, to apply it: He thought in order to act: And the exigencies of a contemplated action reciprocally drew out the guiding principles, and collected the necessary facts. In such a state of things, the mind is wrought up to a wonderful activity. All thought is concrete, all knowledge runs into real life; and all the pressing circumstances and wants of life impel to thought, and seem to be looking about for knowledge and information.

The intellectual development of Lincoln under this discipline may be summed up in three particulars: First, a keen and accurate observation and discernment which grasped facts and truths in their bare and massive reality, estimated their weight and value, perceived their relations and bearing, and the uses to be made of them. This was accompanied with the power of stating them so plainly, and vividly, that what he saw himself he made others see. The power of his discourses and debates did not lie in what is popularly regarded as eloquence, but, in conviction produced by unquestionable realities.

Secondly, a power of clear and straight forward reasoning from secure premises. Lincoln was naturally a logician. Without any training in scholastic logic, or any consciousness of logical forms, he never failed in logical accuracy. The perspicacity of his mind enabled him to look directly through the facts and principles to the conclusion. And so natural and easy was the form of his argument that his hearers seemed to be carried along in the channel of their own thoughts. One thing strongly characterised him, and that was a pervading and quiet consciousness of the strength of his position. He argued from conviction, and felt the truth through his whole soul. Hence he argued without anxiety, and never felt tempted to do any injustice to his opponent, by mistatement, concealment, or sophistry. It has been remarked of him that he generally stated the argument of his opponent with more clearness than he had stated it himself. Discussion with him was a fair and honest battle for the truth.

Thirdly, a power of vivid illustration, and of conveying truths and forming arguments, by anecdotes generally of a humorous character. He had apparently an inexhaustible supply of these. While they amused by the wit and humour which they contained, they often spared the necessity of a formal argument by flashing out the truth at once. He has been severely criticised for indulging this propensity. But it was so much a part of him that he could hardly repress it without ceasing to be himself. In that early rude western life, his genial disposition and native humour led him to converse with the people in this way. It grew into a habit: it characterised him: it was a part of his logic: it was a mode of teaching, a mode of persuasion, a way of subduing enmities, of diffusing kindliness and reawakening good will. To the people, and probably to himself, he would no longer have been Abraham Lincoln, had his flow of anecdotes entirely ceased. A teacher among the Ancients taught by fables and was accounted wise and pertinent. A collection of

2

his fables is still preserved to us. Could a collection of Lincoln's anecdotes be made together with a history of the occasions on which they were uttered, they would probably be found not to be inferior to the fables of Äsop in the force of their truths and the pungency of their wit.

This gift so agreable and useful to others, implied a cheerful and elastic temperament well fitted to endure the anxieties, trials and toils to which he was destined, and which might have crushed him had he been differently constituted.

The intellectual development of Lincoln had, of course, its basis in himself, in a happy natural constitution; but taking form from the conditions and exigencies of his life it qualified him precisely to meet these conditions and exigencies He became thus an eminently practical man in the sphere in which he was placed. But, the general habitude of being thus created, quickness of apprehension, readiness of self-adaptation, and skill in action, formed a preparation for events circumstances and duties which lay beyond that sphere. The same was true of Franklin. Such a man seems to have collected within himself a reserved force ready for ever contingency of human life, ready for every task of duty which Providence may impose.

Doubtless there are others who have gained the same preparation, who do not find the same occasion. Lincoln belonged to a class of men who form the reserved force of society for great emergencies and important duties. He was one of the best specimens of this class. This reserved force is particularly important in a Democracy like our own, where the highest offices are not forbidden to the aspirations of any one. Unworthy men may ofttimes gain the ascendency. But the evil sooner or later finds a limit. There are other spirits at work in the

great community, and the man appears, as by a law of
nature, whom the hour and the duty demand. It was
just in this way, that Lincoln himself came forward in
a higher sphere of action.

There were others in the Republic of equal or of
greater ability, but there could hardly be found one of
greater virtue. It was in his unquestionable integrity
patriotism, humanity, goodness and purity — all combined
that his greatness lay.

Here, as in the case of his intellectual development,
the basis was in himself, in a happy constitution of his
social and moral nature. Those who knew him early,
and who have known him long, and who have known him
intimately in all relations, concur in the testimony,
which they give of his genial, unselfish, kindly, forgiving,
generous and honest nature. He was always true to the
form of character originally impressed upon him: none
of his gifts were suffered to run to waste, to die out,
or to become perverted. In the formative periods of
society there are many and peculiar temptations to evil,
as well as many and peculiar opportunities of doing good.
He appears to have steadfastly resisted the former, and
to have faithfully improved the latter. Amid the tides
of life which were flowing into the great West, he was
a landmark of principle and duty, of upright dealing, of
true philanthropy, of manly independence, of public spirit,
and of patriotic devotion. In his family, he was affectio-
nate and gracious: among his friends, simple hearted and
trustful: among the people at large, a man without guile.
He was not a politician in the too common acceptation
of the term, for he had not the selfish ambition and the
cunning arts of the demagogue. But he was a politician
in the true acceptation of the term, for he aimed to ex-
pound the constitution according to the intention of its

2*

founders, to enlighten the people while he acknowledged
the sovereignty of their will, to promote the public good
by legitimate measures, and to consolidate the Republic
by truth and justice. So transparent were his virtues,
that even his opponents did not deny them. As for
enemies, he had none, except those who were also the
enemies of his country.

Such was Abraham Lincoln ; a product of American Democracy; and a faithful representative of its
principles and its scope, of its power and its bene-
ficence. As all aristocratic lines must have taken their
beginning in common men who acquired distinction
by violence or by illustrious deeds, so he in other times
or in other nations might have been the founder of a
new line of Nobility. Belonging to a country which allows
of no artificial distinctions of rank, which acknowledges
no Aristocracy but what is common to all good and great
men, he will leave an unadorned name to his posterity.
But although unadorned, it cannot lose its innate nobility and royalty as the name of one who vindicated the
rights of man by proclaming liberty and justice to the
slave, and who wisely bravely and faithfully served the
Republic in the days of her greatest peril.

The struggle of America which now closes in triumph
and glory, and with which Lincoln will be forever asso-
ciated, as the great leader, and the patriot-martyr, in its
fundamental elements, is a struggle for the rights of labor.

Labor is the great power of good in the world. God
and nature are always at work. Man, by the labor of
his mind, and by the labor of his hands, improves the
rude world given to him by God and Nature. By the
first he achieves science, art, and all useful inventions.
The labor of his mind guides the labor of his hands. By
the second, he levels the forests and cultivates the earth,

delves into the mines, and constructs implements and machinery, opens highways and spans the rivers with bridges, builds houses and ships, and manufactures all the fabrics of use and beauty. By labor has man changed the face of the earth, made it more beautiful, and filled it with good things.

Endowments of mind, and the power to labor, we possess without our own choice. By voluntary labor we become good, meritorious, and godlike. Among all who are to be valued, cherished, and honored, and to be surrounded with safe-guards and encouragements, nothing seems clearer than that the class of laborers should stand preeminent. And yet the fate of the laborer has generally been a hard fate in our world. The laborers with the mind, although, their great works have eventually compelled the admiration of mankind, and their tombs have been wreathed with garlands; alas! in how many instances have they, while living, been neglected, or persecuted, or given over to withering poverty. The story of genius is an old, sad, and well known story.

The laborers with the hands have been 'still more severely dealt with. From the building of the pyramids to the growing of cotton on southern plantations, what hard centuries of degraded and enslaved labor have passed over the world! In this false state of things, the man of idleness who contributed nothing to the common good; but, who lived upon the fruits of labor exacted with the mailed hand, became the gentleman — the lord: while, the laborer, whose manly industry kept the world alive and produced the wealth of nations, became the serf, the bondsman, the slave. And labor, upon which all depended as the ministering power of all earthly blessings, became a degradation.

It is not surprising that labor broke forth into struggles

for its rights — for the right of free scope to exercise
itself; for the right of appropriating and enjoying its
own fruits; for the right of educating itself and enlarging
the sphere of its enjoyment; for the right to think, to
speak, and to act as God has given this right to all
men; for social and political freedom. On the banks of
Father Rhine are many ruined castles and towers. They
stand there to day monuments of the victorious struggles
of labor against its oppressors. Labor has had its advocates and its heroes, and its rights have been vindicated. Nothing so marks the progress of civilisation, the
spread of christian ideas, and the triumphs of political
economy as the elevation of labor. A nation of enslaved
laborers can never develope its resources to the highest
degrees of National wealth, reach a humane and christian
civilisation, or gain trustful guarantees of perpetuity.
The people really compose the Nation; the body of the
people must always be laborers; the advance of a nation,
therefore, keeps pace with the improvement if its labor-
ing population, whether considered in the light of numbers,
or of productive forces.

With the wise and noble act of the enlightened Czar
of Russia, the enslavement of labor has ceased in Europe.
It now only remains for the different governments to carry
out the benign policy of our age; and, by the universal
diffusion of knowledge, and all wise provisions for encou-
raging and honoring labor, to elevate the masses to the
self conscious worth and dignity which properly belongs
to all men, because they are men.

It is remarkable that in what claimed to be the freest
nation — the great Republic, there should have existed
the most intense and infamous form of enslaved labor.
It did not exist throughout the Republic but only in a
part of it. But it exerted an influence more or less

powerful every where, and was plotting and striving to become universal when the great struggle began. It was slave labor entering the lists against free labor for the possession of the Republic. And when it found it could not at once possess the whole, it aimed to divide, and by division to distract weaken and undermine; and then, having developed itself into a great military power, to conquer the whole, and to conquer in every direction, and find room to spread itself according to its necessities and its ambition.

It formed itself into a system as will a power. It had its philosophy, its creed, and its social theory. Nature had made a distinction of races, and had given to the superior race the right to enslave the inferior. Both races were in their normal condition, when the one possessed the lands, possessed all that was to be possessed, possessed the very persons of the inferior race, and exercised all the political power. The inferior race were to be laborers and nothing more, laborers absolutely governed by their masters.

Labor was a necessity in the world, but it was also a degradation, and therefore belonged to the inferior race. The principle so broadly announced would be applicable to every inferior race. As the ethnological question might ofttimes be difficult to determine, and the ethnological decision might not always be quietly submitted to; in the end, the strong arm would be likely to be appealed to, and the conquered race would become the inferior one. The conquerers would be lords, and the conquered slaves. The doctrine that might makes right would be thus revived; and the reign of violence restored. In such a community labor is utterly dishonored. For any one of the superior race to labor would be to descend to the level of the slave. The prevalence of this sentiment, at the South, produced its fruits in the scorn with which the free laborers of the North were regarded, and spoken of as „Mudsills"; and in the multiplication of poor ignorant and proud men, who claimed idleness as the attribute of gentlemen.

To support this system, Christianity was perverted by new interpretations, free thought and free discussion were prohibited, and the circulation of books guarded; and to shut out more effectually the chances of education to the slave and to bind him to his chattel condition, popular education was frowned upon, and the curse of ignorance entailed upon the poor whites as well as upon the negroes.

The state of society, characterised by its advocates as one of the highest civilisation and refinement, thus produced, presents three classes; an Aristocracy of slaveholders; slave-laborers; and a mass of poor idle and ignorant white men, the material out of which to form an unscrupulous police force, and a host of ferocious soldiery. What is this but a return to feudalism with its worst features, but without its splendour and its romantic chivalry?

In such a state of society there is scarcely any limit to the demoralisation which ensues. The chief right of man — the right of liberty, that which gives value to all other rights, trampled upon in regard to an entire class, and that too a class lying at the foundation of the whole structure of society, must generate a spirit prepared for the commission of any wrong, of any atrocity. The cruelties practised upon the slave, the violation of his domestic sanctities, the reckless sacrifice of his life, naturally followed his degradation to the condition of a chattel — a thing that could be bought and sold. And it was to be anticipated that the habits of wrong and cruelty, formed in this relation, would make their appearance in other relations also. Such men will be violent and cruel to each other when their passions are inflamed. They are impatient of opposition to their opinions and interests. They are ready to tyrannise over any human being. In war they will scruple at no means of accomplishing their purposes, and wreaking their vengeance. In enslaving their fellow men, they have adready made war upon human nature. At what point shall they pause after this?

Northern ideas and principles, the entire frame-work of Northern society are directly opposed to all this. At the North, the rights of labor are fully conceded. Here labor has been educated and honored from the beginning. Here is free labor, free thought, free speech, and free schools — the universal diffusion of knowledge. The institutions of the North are all framed for peaceful and productive labor — labor with the mind, and labor with the hands. The rapid progress of the North, the amazing development of every form of improvement, the vast increase in wealth and its wide distribution, the inventive energy, the agriculture and manufactures, the commerce foreign and domestic, the mining operations, the population pressing into new territories, the multiplication and growth of cities, the development of educational institutions, the free planting of christian churches everywhere, the enterprising and all embracing charities, shew the predominant ideas and the character of the people. They had no interest in war. There was nothing to tempt them to hostile aggressions. Theirs were the conquests and triumphs of peaceful and enriching industry, of knowledge, religion, and charity. They had the wide continent before them, and every man was free to act out his energies. It was a new development of the human race which claimed the sympathies of mankind.

So the South and the North were opposed to each other in their principles of human nature and of human labor. The sublime axiom of human equality and of human rights announced in the Declaration of Independence was practically adopted by the North, and practically rejected by the South.

At the time the Constitution was formed, the viru-' lence of slavery had not fully revealed itself, and it was expected by the framers of that instrument that economical interests would concur with the influences of philanthropy and christianity in removing the one dark evil from our land. But when the improved methods of cotton-cultivation came in, such possibilities of wealth and power were revealed, that cupidity and ambition from that moment proclaimed its perpetuation. It soon became evident that to perpetuate it, it must be spread indefinitely. Slave labor is the most expensive form of labor, and to become profitable must admit of the concentration of numerous laborers upon fresh virgin soils, to ensure large products and rapid returns. Given, a full and constant supply of such soils, and a full and constant supply of slaves, and there is no limit to the accumulation of wealth by the cotton-cultivation. This constant supply of soil and slaves was the problem of the South, which was to be worked out by occupying the territories of the Union with slave-labor, by conquering new territories from without, and by ultimately reopening the slave trade.

The supply of fresh soils in new territories was required not only for the increase of the cotton-cultivation, but also for the maintainance of that already in existence. Under the system of slave-labor, when a soil is exhausted by large and profitable cultivation, it is forsaken, simply, because slave labor is both too unskillful and too expensive to recuperate it. It is a system, therefore, of the constant invasion of nature: exhausting to invade, and invading to exhaust. Whatever be done with the exhausted territory, it can no longer be, profitably, cultivated by slave-labour. This statement is borne out by the declarations of slaveholders themselves, and by the whole history of slavery in America.

If slavery were confined within a given teritory, it would die out from the exhaustion of the soil. The slaveholders determined that it should not die out; on the contrary, that it should be perpetuated and spread into the dimensions of an ever aggressing slave Empire. And first of all, it was necessary that it should have free access to the territories of the Union. Here was the point of direct collision between the North and the South.

To deny it to the territories was equivalent to denying its extension, at all; was to confine it to its old limits and to leave it to the operation of laws which, it was believed, would bring about its extinction.

Without going into a history of this controversy, it is sufficient for our purpose to remark that Abraham Lincoln first became greatly distinguished as a political leader and a political debater, in relation to this question of admitting slavelabor into the free territories of the Union; and that he became President of the United States as the representative of the principle that slavelabor should be admitted into these free territories no more than into the free states themselves. By the decision of the Supreme Court in the Dred Scott case, Congress had no power to prohibit the admission of slavery into the territories; and the implication was strong that slavery might be introduced into the free states, also, like any other property. The entire Government and the Supreme Court were under the controlling influence of the slave power.

There was evidently a conspiracy to make slavery a national institution.

The Republican party, the party which elected Lincoln, was purely a party of the North. The free laborers of the North elected a free laborer of the North to be their representative, as well as the head of the nation, in their great struggle against the progress of slavelabor. His origin, his training, his principles and sympathies, as well as his eminent ability, qualified him for this position. Two years before, in his emphatic language, he had announced the approaching crisis of the Nation: "A house divided against itself cannot stand. I believe that this Government cannot endure permanently half slave and half free. I do not expect the Union to be dissolved — I do not expect the house to fall — but I do expect it will cease to be divided. It will become all one thing, or all the other. Either, the opponents of slavery will arrest the further spread of it and place it where the public mind shall rest in the belief that it is in the course of ultimate extinction, or its advocates will push it forward till it shall become alike lawful in all the states, old as well as new, North as well as South." At the same time, he announced the great principle of the rights of labor, on which he took his stand in the contest: "There is no reason in the world why the negro is not entitled to all the natural rights enumerated in the Declaration of Independance, the rights of life liberty and the pursuit of happiness. I hold that he is as much entitled to these as the white man. He may not be my equal in many respects — certainly not in color, perhaps not in moral and intellectual endowment. But in the right to eat the bread, without the leave of any body else, which his own hand earns, he is my equal and the equal of every living man."

Lincoln and his party designed to vindicate, protect, and secure the rights of labor by political measures peaceful and constitutional. They would effect a revision of the decisions of the Supreme Court by a purification and reorganisation of the Bench. They would reform the national legislation, and the national policy. They would place slavery within the limits assigned it by the constitution, and by the fathers of the Republic, and where, it was hoped, it would ultimately fade away.

But the South did not suffer it to be a peaceful political struggle. The absurd doctrine of State-Sovereignty, and the right of states to secede from the nation, long cherished and not unfrequently spoken out, they now put in practice, upon the election of Lincoln. They plunged the Nation into civil war — a war of the slave power against free labor and the rights of man — the slave Aristocracy of the South against the Democracy of the North.

On the part of the North, it is a war, we say, to vindicate the rights of labor. But in this, it is also a war for liberty in the largest sense, for humanity and justice, for christianity itself.

In estimating the value and the glory of the cause, to which Lincoln devoted himself and to which he has fallen a sacrifice, it is necessary to add one thing more — this war as waged by the North is a war for peace. The line dividing the Empire, which the South proposed to create, from the Free States could be only an imaginary line. Between these regions there are no natural barriers of mountains, rivers, and inland seas. Such barriers are always important to the peace of nations. European nations separated by only an imaginary line, do, indeed, avoid collisions upon their borders; but, it must be recollected, that there is nothing in their respective institutions and personal characteristics to provoke hostility. Thus Prussia and Saxony are separated by only an imaginary line; but the people on either side are substantially the same people, with similar ideas, institutions, and interests. But the line dividing the southern from the northern states, in the proposed distribution of Empire, would be a line marking the boundaries of slave and free labor — the boundaries of ideas and institutions the most opposite and hostile possible. Under one constitution and government, with a policy of compromises, with a fugitive slave-law, with political parties intertwining their interests north and south, with southern influence predominant in the administration of public affairs, the slave power was not content, but, was ever agitating for greater immunities. On the other hand, free labor could not be content under the pressure of its powerful and unscrupulous opponent. The innate hostility of the two to each other could not be repressed. Had the U nion remained undisturbed, the conflict would have been purely moral and political, and would have continued until one party or the other had gained the ascendency. In the language of Lincoln, who contemplated only a peaceful controversy, the opponents of slavery would arrest the further spread of it, or its advocates would push it forward until it should become alike lawful in all the states.

Now, when the Slave-states demanded a division of the Union, whatever may have been their professions, they could not have regarded it as a means of peace, but, as a measure which would give them the advantage in a war which must inevitably ensue. By the election of Lincoln they had lost ground in the moral and political conflict: they, therefore, determined to commit the question to the arbitrament of arms. We have it from their own lips, that they looked for a disruption of the

Free States, as a consequence of secession; and that they expected at once an accession of the North-western states immediately interested in the navigation of the Mississippi.

But wherever the dividing line might be drawn — an imaginary line, say, of fifteen hundred miles, they knew, as well as the Free States, that it must become the fiery line of battle. Slave labor and free labor standing face to face close upon the dividing line, each having its own domain, each under its own banner, no longer held in check by their relations to a common government, with no more fugitive-slave laws and compromises; the proud and arrogant slaveholder, on the one border, eyeing with scorn, contempt, and bitter suspicion, his neighbor the free laborer, on the other border; the free laborer ever feeling himself insulted by the affected aristocratic superiority of the other, with no ground for this claim of superiority but the constant perpetration of what in his eyes was a most infamous crime; the miserable slaves on the one border ever looking over into the other as filled with protectors, and „cities of refuge“ — to them a region of constant hope; — the hearts of the whole mass of slaves in the slave Empire turning to that dividing line, which once crossed, they became free men; the constant flight of slaves, and the eager and fiery pursuit with arms and bloodhounds by men who would not mark narrowly the dividing line; strong police forces patrolling the borders on either side to prevent mutual trespass; a line of fortifications on either side filled with soldiery; stringent regulations as to trade and all intercourse; the products of the free states of the west struggling for exit by the Mississippi chained by the, slave power; all the relations and intercourse of the two nations alive with the mutual jealousies, suspicion, fear, and hate of slave labor and free labor: — What must be the result? Beginning with petty personal collisions, the tide of hostility swells more and more, until armies rush together in battle, and a war begins which can end only in the extinction or triumph of slavery. The geographical unity of our country, and the irreconcilable nature of the opposing principles and institutions render this inevitable. Like the war between Spain and Holland, this war may consume the best part of a century; but there is no point at which it can pause, until, victory decisive and absolute perches on one standard or the other.

Had the government of the United States weakly yielded to secession, the South would have had time to consolidate its government, to collect its strength, and to prepare its front of battle; and, perhaps, by its intrigues to sow dissension among the free states. But the government did not yield, and the war was precipitated by the attack upon Fort Sumpter, and secession became at once bloody rebellion. The war on the part of the South had not now the dignity of a war carried on by an acknowledged government.

Abraham Lincoln, true to his oath of office, took up the defence of the Nation against the armed insurgents. He met the evil in its inception. In the development and progress of this war, he struck at its very principle. In its triumphant close, he sweeps slavery and the slaveholder from the land. The triumph of liberty and humanity is also the triumph of peace. The cause of this war, and the occasion of all war, in the future, is removed.

There never has been, and it is not conceivable that there ever can be, any occasion of war between the free United States. There never has been, there never can be, any occasion of war between the states of New England; between New England and New York; between

Pennsylvania and Ohio, between Illinois and Indiana; or
between Iowa and Wisconsin. The interests of the Free
States are so completely identified, and their brotherhood so perfect, that we might as well look for occasions
of war between the different shires of England. Now,
let all the States become free States, and the conditions
of peace are fulfilled for the whole land. Then Pennsylvania will have no more occasion of war with Virginia
than with Ohio; Massachusetts no more occasion of
war with South-Carolina than with Connecticut. Still
more, the entire United States become now a great
peaceful power in relation to the whole world. There
are statesmen in Europe who have looked upon the success of the South and the destruction of the Union as
important to the peace of the World. Has the division
of Europe into numerous states preserved the peace of
Europe? Were America divided into several nations, there
would be standing armies, the art of war would be
cultivated, and a warlike spirit would be kept alive.
Had the South prevailed, it would, unquestionably, have
been a great, a ferocious, an oppresive military power.
But, let us have free states — united free states, from
the northern lakes to the gulf of Mexico, and we dwell
in peace with each other, and with the whole world.
War is not the normal condition of nations. Men are
formed into nations not, that by an union of strength
they may destroy their fellow men, and impoverish the
earth; but, that by the united labors of their minds
and hands they may improve the earth, improve
their own condition, and do their part to benefit mankind. Nations highly civilized and in a prosperous
condition, are reluctant to leave the blessings of
peace for the toils and hazards of war. How happy they

are to return from war to the blessings of peace! War is the choice only of Barbarians.

With the works to be accomplished on our continent, in agriculture, manufactures, and commerce; the fair fields to be won, the wealth to be gained; the arts of civilisation and refinement to be cultivated; the social and political happiness to be achieved under our free institutions; what temptations have we to destroy each other, or to invade the peace of other nations? We are a nation of free laborers working for our own good, and for the good of the world. Beneficient industry — industry in all that promotes human welfare, is the principle of our national life, the secret of our growth and prosperity. Nothing could have interrupted our career, or thrown a cloud over our destiny, but such an accident as slavery — accident we may call it, for it was forced upon us in our colonial state, and did not grow up out of ourselves — the accident of a disease attacking the very seat of life and withering our strength. If war be the reaction which effects our cure, we must submit to it; but when the cure is effected, a repetition of the reaction would become only another form of disease.

Our national health restored, we return to our natural destiny, peace and the arts of peace.

If Abraham Lincoln be a crowned martyr in the cause of free labor, of liberty in the largest sense, of humanity, justice, and christianity, we add another splendour to his crown when we are permitted to say, he was also a martyr in the cause of peace. Nothing could be more grateful to his own gentle and merciful spirit than to interpret his mission as one of peace on earth and good will among men.   ⸙

It remains to consider the wisdom and fidelity with

which he fulfilled his trust. The great principle which guided Lincoln in his administration of the government during the tremendous struggle in which its very existence was involved, was, that he was the servant of the people and the representative of their sovereignty. The war was not his war; it was the war of the people, the war of free labor. His was not the prower to carry on the war. He was not a despot with a standing army, obedient to his will. The war must be carried on by the people — by the free laborers of the North. He, indeed, had authority to order a conscription, he was commander in chief. But he well knew that if the hearts of the people were not in the work the strength and vigor necessary to accomplish it would be wanting. The North was also divided into parties. There were sympathisers with the South, there were even traitors on the soil of freedom. It was necessary that the people should declare themselves; that they should commit themselves unequivocally to the great cause. There is no reason to believe that he ever doubted the people, or that his confidence in the result was ever staggered. Any apparent delay or hesitation was not the result of weakness, but of a determination not to impair, by any assumption on his part, the consciousness of responsibility and power, on the part of the people. It is a beautiful feature in his character — a rare feature, and one that stamps him with true greatness — that while in the darkest days of the struggle he was cheerful, unmoved, and trustful; in the hour of his greatest triumph, when by an overwhelming majority he had been called the second time to the Presidential Chair and all his principles and his administration had been sealed with the popular approbation, when the armies were victorious, the rebellion crushed, and he entered the rebel capital as a conqueror, he never

3*

for a moment lost the balance of his mind, exhibited no
elation, pride, arrogance, or vindictiveness, and was never
less lordly and tyrannical. In the zenith of his power and
fame he was the same unpretending Abraham Lincoln; as
much the servant of the people as at the beginning of his career.
In carrying out the principle of eliciting expressions of
the popular will, he first called for 75,000 volunteers, for
the purpose of repossessing the government of the fortresses
arsenals and other public property which the rebels had
seized. Not only 75,000 obeyed the call, but hundreds
of thousands appeared ready to follow. Again he called
for half a million, as the war swelled in its dimensions,
and 700,000 sprang to arms. At one period of the war
the number who offered themselves was so great, that
the volunteering, perhaps injudiciously, was checked.
Throughout the entire war, conscription has been resorted
to, only, to a limited extent; and principally at the later
periods. The payment of high bounties does not take
away from the grandeur of the movement, but rightly
considered reveals a high sense of justice in the American people. They believed that the families of soldiers
in the field, ought to be provided for. A large portion
of the bounties and wages paid to soldiers was transmit-
ted to wives and children, or to others dependent upon
them. There are instances where poor men have bought
a house and land with their bounty-money as a home
and support for their families, and have gone to the war
never to return. The patriotism which led them to sacrifice their lives, was not less genuine that it was mingled with a tender care for those who were left behind.
It was but just in those who did not share the perils of
battle to enable him who went into the field to make
this provision for those who looked to him for support.
The government has been inspired by the popular feeling

in the provision it has made for the families of the slain:
36,000 widows are already on its pension roll. Indeed
the display of philanthropy is one of the most remarkable features of our great struggle. The Sanitary Commission has raised, by voluntary subscription, more than thirty
millions of dollars for the relief of wounded and sick
soldiers. Its agents have been found on every battle field,
in every hospital. The Christian Commission has provided the camps and hospitals with books, and has brought
religious consolation to the wounded, sick, and dying. In
all this, the hearts of the people responded to the call
of the President, and proved to him that they were ear-
nest in the great cause, as the cause of God and humanity.

The President applied, also, his principle of waiting on
the manifestations of the popular sentiment, to the great
question of emancipation, in reality the fundamental
question. His own sentiments on the subject of slavery
had long before been fully declared. No one could doubt
that he regarded its extinction as necessary to the perpetuity of the Republic, as well as an act of justice. But
as President of the United States, in his civil capacity,
he had no power to abolish it. Nor had Congress any
power over it. The power to abolish it was reserved to
the states in which it existed. It was only after rebellion had taken place that, as commander in chief, he
could proclaim emancipation as a military necessity.
Perhaps, in the end, the judgment will be arrived at,
that the act of rebellion itself dissolved the relation of
master and slave. But so widely did prejudices prevail
against Abolitionism, and so bitter had been the strife of
parties, that the thunder of many battles was necessary
to clear up the political atmosphere, to enable the people
to see the full merits of the contest. Lincoln had full

assurance that the heart of the North was opposed to
slavery. He knew that the time would come when the
tide of popular conviction and energy would be at the
full. He would not forestall the mighty action of the nation by the weaker action of an individual, even after the
military necessity, in his own judgment, had arrived. He
was not mistaken: the time came: and when he proclaimed
emancipation it was not a mere display of his own
authority, of doubtful success; but an expression of the
sentiment and purpose of the majority of the people.
His adherence to this principle may appear to many to
have involved him in perilous delays. Certainly, it de-
prived him of the quick decision and the energy of a dic-
tator: But it secured the Republic from the danger of
perishing by its deliverers, after it had triumphed over
its foes. All must acknowledge, too, that however slow
he may have been in arriving at his conclusions, and in
maturing his purposes, it was never necessary for him
to retrace his steps, nor did he ever waver or falter in
execution.

This remarkable and leading characteristic of his public measures, arose not only from a just appreciation of
what belongs to the office of the Chief Magistrate of a
Republic; but, sprung also from the very depths of a
nature where modesty and firmness were rarely and ad-
mirably balanced. This trait was no less conspicuous in
his readiness to receive counsel, while his ultimate decisions were made with manly independence, and were
unflinchingly carried out.

In the prosecution of the war, there was no lack of
soldiers, or of arms and munitions. The patriotism, wealth,
and energy of the nation supplied these. Nor was there
a deficiency of educated officers and engineers. Our military schools, and, above all, the National Academy at

West-Point on the Hudson river, had afforded admirable
training to a large number; part of whom held appoint-
ments in the army, and many who had retired from the
army stood ready to obey their country's call in any
emergency. The consequence was, that not many months
elapsed, after the commencement of the war, before the
nation, roused all the more by the disaster at Bull's Run,
produced in the field a large, well appointed, and well
disciplined army under the command of General M'Clellan.
There were armies also at other points. Our experience
in the Mexican war, and in the present war, has proved
to us, that with educated officers, our volunteers, from the
habit of quick self-adaptation acquired in American life,
are very rapidly moulded into soldiers by military drill.
The want that we experienced at the beginning of the
war was the want of a great commander, one who should
unite with a military education all those qualities which
are expressed by the one word — *strategy*. An army is
a force: the genius of a great commander becomes the
law to direct it to the accomplishment of its proper ends.
Our great commander in previous wars was disqualified
by age. We had to find a new one; and one competent
to command armies of unexampled magnitude, operating
upon a theatre of unexampled extent, and amid difficul-
ties that presented new problems in the art of war. For
two years the war may be called a war of experiments
to find a general. At last he was found; and with him,
as always happens, appeared others fitted to act with
him. It is one of the prime qualities which makes a
great commander that he knows how to select his subordinates. It was a rare merit in Lincoln that he succeeded
in finding the great commander. He had no favorites
to advance: he had within his own bosom no jealous fears
to propitiate: he was cool and sagacious in his judgment,

and impartial and firm in his decisions. Nevertheless, he
had to bear with mediocrity and pretension, when surrounded with popular favor, to an extent that might have
worn out the patience of any other man; and was compelled to face disappointments which, beyond the wound-
ing of his own heart, involved loss of reputation to worthy
men, serious disasters to the army, discouragement to
the nation, and exposure to the criticisms of excited and
alarmed patriots, and the censures of enemies lying in
wait for his ruin. But, coolly, calmly, patiently, bravely
he persevered; losing no hope, and only collecting fresh
resolution from every failure. And so the mighty war
went on, until at length amid its ever changing fortunes,
like the prophet seeking for the "Lord's anointed", he
discerned the Hero of the war. It grew out of his wisdom, his modesty, his magnanimity, that whenever he
appointed a general, he supplied him ungrudgingly with
all the material of war, and committed the manage-
ment of the war to him without reserve. He had
done so in the case of M'Clellan and other generals.
And he never interfered except in the utmost exigency,
or when results tought him that a change in the command
had become necessary. When he had placed Grant in
command, it became obvious to him and to the whole
nation that experiments were at an end, and that the
proper man had found his proper place. Had Lincoln
been more ambitious, and less patriotic, he might have
envied the great leader of our armies, and have sought
to appropriate to himself a share of the glory of victory.
But there was in him no trace of such a disposition.
He neither affected to direct the military movements,
nor to claim the merit of success. He supplied whatever was necessary with the whole energy of the government, and left the general undisturbed to plan the mo-

vements, and to lead the armies. It was singular good fortune for our country that the two men, in whose hands her fates seemed to lie, were so similar and congenial in the modesty, unselfishness, and magnanimity of their natures, in their patriotic intentions, in their clear comprehension of the scope of the war, and of what it involved to our country and to mankind, and in their immoveable determination to close the war, only, with the proclamation of liberty to the slave made good, and the Union restored.

What Mr. Lincoln was in his relations to his generals, he was also in his relations to his cabinet. He was neither jealous, suspicious nor arbitrary. Maintaining his proper positon as the head of the government, and never evading his own responsibilities; he, at the same time, accorded to every one around him the fullest opportunities to fill out the functions which belonged to his department, to bear the burden of its duties, and to win all the honors of wise and successful service rendered to the Nation.

The remark has frequently been made that the war would not have been protracted through so many years had there been a large standing army maintained by our government. This remark is not well considered. As a peaceful nation occupying a position isolated from the great powers of the earth, we had no use for a large standing army. Besides, such an army would have been one of the most appalling sources of danger upon the breaking out of the rebellion. The machinations of the conspirators which embraced the seizure of the forts and arsenals, and the corruption of officers of the government civil and military, in case of a large standing army, would have directed their main efforts, through years of preparation, to gain a control of the whole military power,

Accomplishing this, they would have regarded their work as done. The probabilities of success in this scheme would have been great. A standing army is necessarily more or less separated from the people, and grows into a peculiar community, with sentiments, views and aims, removed from popular interests and the arts of peace. War is its normal employment; and it always looks forward to war as affording the opportunities for action, and for the gains and honors after which it naturally aspires. Of all forms of authority that of its officers is the only one immediately felt and respected; where all the subordinates centre in a chief, in whom the ability to command assumes the charm of majesty. A standing army is a despotic organisation, and is despotic in its sympathies. In a Republic it is prone to degenerate into a force arrayed against the people. The Roman Empire grew out of the Roman Republic by the force of a military organisation. Had the slave power of the South succeeded in drawing around it the sympathies of a powerful standing army, the freemen of the North would have had a still sterner work before them than the last four years have revealed; and their complete and secure triumph could have been achieved only by the utter destruction of the despotic army as well as of slavery, as it can now be achieved only by the destruction of the military power of the South and of slavery. The true soldiers of a free people are the people themselves, who go from the plough to the battle field, and return from the battle field to the plough. A military training may enter into the common education of such a people; but their own patriotic hearts, and their own strong arms form their mightiest and safest defence.

It was not a standing army we required. We required only that which every nation requires in time of

war, and which has so often turned the balance of victory
— we required a great heroic general. Standing armies
perfectly drilled do not ensure this. The history of war
is rich in examples of disciplined armies defeated by
inferior numbers through the strategy and energy of an
original genius in the art of war. But it is only in the
experience of war arousing human energies that the Hero
appears. It was the experience of war that gave to
Prussia a Frederic and a Blücher. It was the experience
of war that gave to England a Cromwell, a Nelson and
a Wellington. It was the experience of war that gave
to France a Napoleon and his marshalls. It was the
experience of war that gave to America a Washington.
It is the experience of war, now again, which has given
us a Grant.

Lincoln trusted in the voluntary uprising of a free
people, and he trusted in the true and great hearted
commander, whom the experience of the war had revealed to him. But more than all, he trusted in God. He
believed in a Providence that watches the fall of a
sparrow, and the conflicts of nations. In his public
speeches and official proclamations, and in his familiar
conversations he evinced his belief and trust in a God
of truth and justice. He devoutly believed that the
cause of his country was one of truth and justice, and
therefore dear to God. His piety was unpretending like
all his virtues, but like them, too, laid in the foundations
of his being. Hence, whatever trials he and his country might be called to pass through, he faltered not in
his confidence of a happy ending. Justice might demand
that the wealth accumulated by unrequited labor should
be swept away, that every drop of blood drawn by the
lash should be atoned for, by a corresponding drop drawn
by the sword; but, he saw beyond the days of trial and

the bloody penance, the days of peace and brotherhood returning; a purified constitution and a regenerated people, a reconstructed Union resting securely on the rights of man; sister states embracing each other from ocean to ocean; his country one and undivided free and independent, stretching its peaceful and prosperous existence through the coming centuries, and collecting around itself the sympathies and hopes of mankind. It was for his whole country, the South as well as the North, the East as well as the West, that he labored, and dreamed dreams of peace prosperity and glory. He had accomplished the first part of his work — he had destroyed slavery and the military power of the South; he was about to enter upon the second part — the part so congenial to his nature — to reconstruct and unite, to revive, to heal, and reanimate the nation, when he was laid low by an act of vengeance which civilized and christian nations will not justify even when a tyrant is its object, and which fills them with horror and dismay when a just man and a friend of humanity becomes its victim. No one doubts the greatness of the loss: no one palliates the enormity of the crime.

But the work which Lincoln left unfinished will not remain unfinished. The man who takes his place was, like him, a humble laborer originally; like him was selfeducated, and educated by the exigencies of a life spent in the public service, educated like Franklin and Cobden; a man who as a poor white of the south has felt the iron heel of the slave power, and who during this rebellion has had experience of the vindictiveness of that power, as well as of losses on the field of battle; a man of noble gifts, and pure patriotic aims. We shall miss the gentle and forgiving spirit of Lincoln, and a ray of sunshine will fade from the capitol with his benignant smile. His manly sense, his experienced wisdom, and his playful humour formed a combination too rich and original to be easily replaced. But his very death proves that the sterner justice which may characterise his successor may be demanded for the completion of his work. His principles live; his example cannot be forgotten; the great cause for which he died presses the more upon us in consequence of his death; and the New President, and a united people, while they touched his bier, have sworn in their hearts, that his work shall not remain unfinished.

As for him, death came to him in the ripeness of his years, his virtues, and his fame. There is not a stain upon his fair and honored name. We look upon him as an honest man — God's noblest work. In him we have nothing to regret, but that we have lost him.

> „So live that when thy summons comes to join
> The innumerable caravan, that moves
> To that mysterious realm, where each shall take
> His chamber in the silent halls of death,
> Thou go not like the quarry-slave at night,
> Scourged to his dungeon, but, sustained and soothed
> By an unfaltering trust, approach thy grave,
> Like one who wraps the drapery of his couch
> About him, and lies down to pleasant dreams.‟

So Abraham Lincoln lived and died. Although the drapery of his couch was stained by his pure patriot blood, no one doubts that it was wrapped about a peaceful conscience, and that he laid down to pleasant dreams of „life and immortality.‟

This good man will have his reward both here and in the other world. Here, one of the bright stars in the galaxy of history, he will be recorded among Heroes, Patriots and Martyrs. By his countrymen, his memory will be everlastingly honored, and tenderly cherished. His name will take its place beside the glorious name of

Washington: one laid the foundations of American liberty: the other completed the work, by banishing slavery from the land. Together they will go down to all the coming generations among "the few the immortal names that were not born to die."

In that other world to which he has gone, he will join "the noble company of the Martyrs" and of "the Just made perfect."

Blessed are the dead who die in the Lord: — They rest from their labours, and their works do follow them.